Unknowable Things

by

Kerry Trautman

ROADSIDE PRESS

copy-right

Editor: Michele McDannold

Roadside Press
Meredosia, IL

Contents

for xxx

you cannot touch us
we cannot touch you
we are untouchable

Drops

He closed the screen door, stepped
into rain that smelled like worms.

I could only think I wanted
those drops to drizzle
from my scalp to eyebrows.

There's these unexpected
lumps in you, he said
through the screen.
Like the ridges and pits in
the bottom of hot tubs.

Referring, maybe, to
my need to gulp water—
if it tastes good, very cold,
gulp till I gasp for
my next breath,
letting my blouse get dribbled,
even if it's silk, which it
never was.

Through the screen I said,
I'm just thirsty.

Eggs Fried by a Friend's Father

No toast, I said, not too hungry.
Then what will you dip in your eggs?

But I could not imagine
any dipping into pale rubber curds.

My plate appeared—
cartoon eyeballs,
oil-painted breasts,
silly rounded contrast
so brazenly biological.

Crisped feather edges still sizzling
their minute buttery brownness
surrounding milky, stilled puddles
with their rain-washed marigolds.

He handed me a triangle of wheat.
I watched him rupture his
globule to glossy ooze,
a droplet dripping on its way to his mouth.

I grimaced, mimicked
the crunch and flow—

sunrise thunder,
a goldfinch flock alighting
backdropped by lightning,
a gold, silk ball-gown washed out to sea.

I tried to douse any chicken-y images,
babies in general,
life as its whole,

allow the fatty velvet draping
my tonsils and tongue to be

only morning's oiled light.
It would be ok.

Iceland Green

Mom, you always told me that
Greenland is icy and
Iceland is green.
Green with birch trees and moss.
Because of the geysers
and steam
under the crust
under the green.

Then you should have known
about him,
about the green,
about the depth of green
and roots planted in crust,
in lava crust that crumbles loose
and gives way
and explodes
with a little pressure from
underneath.

Mom, you should have
known,

should have told me

more

about Iceland.

Pretty

Most of us are not undeniably, unanimously beautiful, but the day she wore her hair in a high high ponytail so the ends—blonder from summer's swimming—hung beside her cheeks, she felt pretty. And when the bus stopped at the junior-high to get the older kids and a mob of sidewalk boys cat-called toward her face in the shut bus window, made sex gestures, flicked their tongues, she smiled. She knew she was supposed to be shocked, pissed, roll her eyes, pretend she didn't see them, but it was her first taste of pretty.

Dysmorphia

This junk-drawer carting my delicious
brain around, my heart, my working hands,
other used-to-be-useful bits.
Conveying things I don't intend.

There is *Mulholland Drive* on tv, then
there is the tv itself.

One two three four
step two three four
never does my body whirl in
proper dancing rhythm, but it
lumbers this way and that.

It's some miracle when my abdomen
shudders with weeping, because for once
I and my body unite.

There is *Mulholland Drive* on tv, then
there is Los Angeles itself.

Fluids and solids pass in and out

sometimes including blood.

There is the eggshell splashed
with chicken shit, then
there is the beautiful goo of
omelets or genoise.

One two three four
turn two three four
never will my muscles push the
rest of me in unison with
someone else I'm watching.

There is *Mulholland Drive* on tv, then
there is Naomi Watts herself.

There is this sack of slush ambling
between my rooms, then
there is the RAM,
then there is a zodiac,
creases across palms,
something else.

Spider-Man

The comic book man with a U of shelves
in the back of the used bookstore
ate black olives from the can, with
a fork brought from home for that purpose.
The can's gouged open-lid
perched up, perilously sharp,
attached by a millimeter of bent metal.

He skimmed a Spider-Man, stopped
at a panel with a close-up, startled Mary Jane.
He wanted to climb the spokes of her iris,
set it spinning like a hamster wheel.

Earlier, a twelve-year-old girl
came in for the newest Spider-Man.
And the day before an older girl—
old enough that he felt ok watching
her moving through the shelves.

In high-school, his sister tried
to watch Superman with him.
She asked why he lived in ice, said she

didn't get it, said his room smelled like
socks, Doritos and Mom's Jergens lotion.

The man ran a fingertip down the straight
stapled spine of a Batman—the hero's brow
glaring at Catwoman's blackened burden of
breasts, elongated thigh muscles outlined white
on black. He knew how the ink would smell
if he pressed his face to the pages.

He hoped no more girls would bother him
in the shop, assumed they had only
come because of boyfriends or brothers,
felt like he didn't have what they wanted,
that they didn't know what they wanted,
that there had been some mistake,
that they should go.

He chewed his last olive, chasing it
with a swallow from a Pepsi can—
sweet after salt—wishing
the olives were stuffed with something.

Shell

She collects seashells

because they seem to

need her

laying pink

fragile on

too-hot sand

or being licked always

drowned

by salt wave foam

because the little animals

that hid inside

are dead

and can not

pinch

or run.

Suction

He avoided jealousy, telling
himself, *some folks just*
sweat more than others,
misting his succulents though
they didn't need it, and that's
why she'd given them to him.
He remembered the two of them,
puncturing virgin clay, trowling,
turning in bone meal.
He'd watered them in with
soft gurgles. She'd flushed
rich soil from under her purple
nails, rubbed in lotion,
sucked cantaloupe wedges, wetting
her lipcorners, said,
they won't need much,
unless things get severe.

Pear

I ate the pear deep as I could
through its smooth goldness,
but not so deep as to
strike the brown mush
the core had, hidden, become.

It would have been,
I think, cheating,
to have knifed away
the best of the flesh, like
filleting a trout,

would have neglected
this wet contact, this
toothing and tease of
how far can I go
before it's all ruined after all.

Because, Brian

I liked you at first, because your dad fixed a flat on my mom's Pontiac in his robe, and because of your black jelly bean eyes and big-toothed laugh, and because you almost almost rubbed my thigh. But I bought off-the-shoulder homecoming velvet for someone else, because of your seaweed smell, because of the taste of our one kiss—wet with salts of sweat and Fritos, because it was October and you were nothing, because we were sixteen.

Stray

Was it cruel to have lured the stray cat

these weeks closer to my fingertips,

to teach him petting?

It was a new thing—involuntary

joy on skin terms.

Fur can't help that it's reached-for.

When I had asked the older boy's sister

for his number

she warned

he's sometimes not nice to girls.

The cat cries at the door now

for more than just a bowl of food.

The boy was patient with me,

clasping my button fly.

It was a new thing—him hearing *wait.*

It was a new thing—me being clambered-upon.

Small bodies should be born

knowing what

love feels like on skin terms.

Nights are long

with only wind smoothing haunches.

Is it worth it to crouch,

inch forward toward the dish of a palm?

If this doesn't work,

he warned himself and me and unknown others,

I'll go back to the way I was.

Purring is involuntary, internal.

Claws are internal except

when they are externalized.

What rule did I break by ending it?

What reward did I owe his try at patience?

What continuance do fingertips owe other skin?

Is heartbreak more or less

humane than starvation?

Body as Bird as Body

As a wren, she shrunk into shrubbery.
But not as wren—
no brief wings to shudder skyward.

As a starling, she insinuates herself
into murmurations, a lost-ness of black
on blue on black on blue.

As a barn owl, imperceptible
shadows in rafters.
But not as owl—not sparing the meat.

As a heron, twiggy stillness
sculpturing, obvious above
duckweed and cattails.

As a peahen, beige
full of eggs
behind blue fans of eyes.

As a wren, air barely
exerts beneath.
But not as a wren—of soil.

Store-bought Cookies

She ate oversweet cookies enough
to be ashamed of, thinking,
Damn him. Him just one more thing
to be unsure of—like the false
alarm of foreboding clouds,
the symmetry or not of butterflies' wings,
the doneness of a baking
breadloaf's deepest soft insides.

These cookies, she knew.
These crumbs sanding her cleavage,
these chocolate chips re-softened
by her lips' heat,
these sweet starches brittle
between her teeth,
these things she knew
when confronted with them,

with their uniform rows
nestled in their plastic tray.
She knew how to slit open the wrapping,
knew how many would satisfy,

how many would make her feel ill,

how they felt inside her—

the same each

and every time.

To a Friend Who Moved to Florida

I slice these mangos, knowing
they would kill you.
The one good thing about your being gone.

Were you here
last-minute drop-ins would
set me into panic, spraying
kitchen countertops, thinking
which door handles might my
mango hands have palmed.

I won't try to rhyme
anaphylaxis.

My knife glides through with that slight
drag-scrape at fibrous bits along the pit
and you are here
reminding me that
you are not here.

You are in a new home with
lime and orange groves

with Meyer lemon trees.
Risking panthers, snakes,
and beach cafes with mango smoothies—
but none my fault.

I lay six halves flat-side-down, fillet
the redgold leather skin from round the mounds
and it will be ok.

Juice can compromise my cutting board.
I won't be slicing anything else for you.

I won't try to rhyme
epinephrine.

Your throat, a dozen
states away, is open
wide and wet in humid May
your lungs inflate despite
the orange sweet I swallow.

Bathrooms Are for Bathing

Her foot in the sink.

My mom made me start in eighth grade.

She shaved a stroke of shinbone from ankle up to knee,

Said no boys'd pick me.

She rinsed the razor, water streaming between her toes. Green plastic tumbler with vodka, two ice cubes, on the counter.

Did I want to be picked?

Brick polish chipped on her nails. She sipped.

In high school it was funny not to.

Big toe garnished with black curl hairs. I wondered if she'd do those too. She sipped.

Little pleated skirts. Roll down the white kneesox and POOF!

She laughed, splot of foam shaken from razor to mirror. She didn't wipe it.

Just us girls, so who cared?

She shaved slowly over the curves of her knee, then behind it. Stretching calf streaked wet with lather specked with stubble.

They couldn't make rules about that.

She rinsed the leg, dried with a dingy blue towel, and it wasn't her leg anymore.

Earlier

If Adam's other ribs had become other women too, would Eve have learned earlier shame for her body, compared the height of her breasts, the lushness of her hair, firmness of thighs, Cain or Abel's stretching of her skin, covered herself earlier with only the glossiest fronds, tucked bright orchids behind her ear, found earlier a method for tempting Adam?

Abstract

Because he'd painted it for her—
stretching the canvas, sized for hanging
over her sofa, away from direct sun—
because he'd avoided reds, knowing
she gets anxious around red and all its
unseemly, private connotations,
she tried. She tried for days to like it.

She tried to force order into its random
brushstrokes, tried to imagine why
this turquoise streak here and not there,
this ochre there, not here.

Like a Rorschach, the gold and olive smear
in the corner became the steel-roofed shed
behind her parents' house, where
a neighbor-boy taught her to tongue kiss.
The deep green near the center—
a broken-necked tropical bird.
Each element became anything,
anything other than pieces of him, of them,
abstractions and nothing more.

24

She wondered how the man she knew

could have left the straight-lined,

marine blue splotch in one corner,

a splotch where he, working on a flat surface,

had obviously dropped his brush,

its dirtied handle stamping its impression.

The man she remembered would have growled,

thrown the ruins to the corner.

Instead, after months without their speaking,

he'd driven the painting to her back door,

left it exposed for her to find,

still bloodied though without red.

And now she searched it for why—

after months without a brush, without

coming home with new tubes clenched in

his fists, eager to spread them,

without pouring her wine, lighting her,

grabbing her by her upper arms to pull her

to his mouth—why now? Why this?

Kitchens Are for Cooking

I didn't want the baby,

she told me, waiting for
the hollandaise to foam.
I watched her arms reach for the whisk.

So I went to Toronto with the old painter.
He had a spare room.

She minced four cloves of garlic,
finely, by hand.
I heard rain.

There was a full bottle of whiskey
on the nightstand each morning.
Till I lost the baby, and still after.

She crumbled some feta
on a salad of kale and dried cranberries.
I memorized the red of the berries.

He started coming in my room at night.

I'd pretend to stay asleep.

She buttered her Calphalon pan.
It sizzled and smoked orange.
I thought about sunsets.

It was good whiskey.

She checked the portabellos in the oven,
heat wafted over us, and purple light.
I let the heat in through my teeth.

After I came home,
I moved from whiskey to wine.

I dipped my finger in the hollandaise.
She wanted me to taste it.

We need cheddar,

she said, pouring two plastic cups
full of zinfandel,

sharp, sharp cheddar.

Staying

He checked his lover
into rehab
and she may or may not
stay.
And while he
wishes her better, he
cannot help but wonder
whether she will come back,
and whether she will be
too strong.
Cannot help but think
of his perennial bed—
how he had chosen the
Gaillardia, Russian Sage,
Golden Marguerite,
because he could leave them,
because they were just fine
all on their own,
and how he later resented
their vigor despite him.
Cannot help but think,
as he eats pasta from cans

and goes to bed cold at ten,

he cannot help but think

that he cannot help her now.

Cannot hold her hair.

Cannot feed her sips of water,

dab her lips

with a cool, damp towel.

The Lover in the Cafe

The Lover is back,
home from Chicago,
sitting at the corner table,
with a notebook,
chewing the end of her pen,
pretending she hadn't driven
ninety on the turnpike
to arrive that much sooner,
watching her old girlfriend wait on tables,
watching her smile at customers,
thinking the smile is brighter now,
like candy,
bigger, more real,
wishing it wasn't.
The Lover watches,
thinks the old girlfriend looks thinner,
same skirt, but it's looser
drapes on her hip-bones,
as if to remind her they exist,
remind her of cupping them
soft and tight in her palms.
The Lover thinks the old girlfriend's hair
is shorter—nice,

maybe someone asked her to cut it,

smoothing it for her,

tucking it back behind her ears

because it never stayed there,

because hair never stays

the way you need it to.

2/3 Water

He neglected leggy philodendrons on his desk, noting their dry soil as he tapped his pencil, picked at his nails. Everything, even skin, heals eventually. He could still smell salt. He chose the apartment for its view—a brick wall— preferring crumbled mortar, precarious mourning dove nests, to lakes or oceans—places too vast with too much space to learn to hide. No one could need that much water.

Tea and Cake

As if it was nothing but a matter of thirst,
she gulped her tea, hot, gripping
the mug handle in her fist, like a child
whose grasp could save her from being
swept off in a mass of strangers.

But she knew the brewed herbs,
soothing as they were, and of earth,
couldn't sluice away his gone face.
The tea, unsweet, seething in her throat
could never provide enough heat.

There should have been milk, but today,
sniffing the jug, she had recoiled,
and since it was spoiled used it to bake
a coffee cake, but with tea instead, because
he always said coffee would yellow her teeth.

She thought baking would help—
the cinnamon cover traces of his smell,
the whirring of the beaters drown
the phantom *clinks* of him stirring his tea.
What isn't healed by warm streusel?

Baking One Potato Warms the Kitchen Just as Well as Baking Two

She forked one charred bit of flaky skin and
thought how hundreds of years ago everyone, always
must have smelled a little bit like fire.

She took a mouthful of the grainy, ivory fluff
right from the steaming center,
glossed by a rivulet of melted butter.
The flesh fell to her stomach with a starchy thud—
the hollow weight of the needing of more.

She pulverized a grain of kosher salt between her left molars,
setting saliva into action.
She thought of juice, from fruit,

from the North Star cherries she would pick
every two June days from her dwarf, backyard tree,
robins chiding her from rooftops.
Stupid birds—didn't they realize that they
would always get the highest fruits?

Rose Window

Lining cherry tomatoes red in a row on her moonlit windowsill, popping the one without its green leaftop through the disposal rubberflaps with a soft *thomp*, angry sighing at the third fruit from the left which kept rolling toward the edge, shooing a fruit-fly, a pink rose from the bush out under the window waved in the wind, just barely a petal visible in the glass, and she jumped, hand on her heart thump, scared something had tried to get inside.

Scrap

3=how many times

I've traced the numbers he scrawled

on a scrap of paper near the keyboard.

4=the number of 8s with

their doubled bellies

clowning atop each other.

69=my zodiac

pinched into $369.32,

reddening the neighboring 3s.

5=the small man with a hat

lolling in the low left corner.

Where had those 5 dollars gone?

Can they amount to much

without a woman there, hatted, beside,

strolling in pairs some April 15th,

highlighting each other's assets?

2=the one curved hook that is a pair,

poised seven times,

within columns—

digits awaiting compilation

transforming one another.

1=the time I leaned to the desk,

sniffed the white paper,

hoping for his fingertips—

only dry ink of occupation,

dim recall of trees.

7=the peace in the pieces left behind.

2,4,6 of the small slashed 7s.

Look at them all

balancing themselves there on the scrap.

Will they pirouette?

Will they drop?

Pixie Cut

With left fingertips
she tucks
phantom hair behind
her left ear
as she's talking—
only grazing nailtips
over tufted scalp,
fingerpads maybe missing
the slipping into place of
what used to be.

She used to climb the frontyard redbud tree
unafraid to skin knees, shins
red as lipstick.

Her great-grandmother once was kept home
from the church carnival for having
rouged her knees.

She swipes right fingertips
across her brow
left to right

to whoosh away bangs

which once clung

to lashes,

undrape her face.

Her husband will not be

coming back.

When climbing redbud trees

one might get spiders in one's hair

or bits of twig.

Her great-grandmother was told,

when she bobbed her hair,

that she would never find a husband.

He used to split her hair in two halves,

smooth it down over her clavicles,

slip it aside, trace her clavicles with

the tip of his tongue.

With a swipe of an axe, a branch or

trunk is hacked. With vibration of blades

a razor shaves to roots,

red lips new nucleus of the face.

Her great-grandmother planted the
redbuds with branches in mind.

She traces
her collarbones
with the tip of
her lipstick tube.

When climbing redbuds,
one might get blossoms in one's hair.

Out the Window

And so the poem starts as many others—
at the kitchen sink, as peaches drip down
elbow to drain, bite after bite, my eyes
forward-faced ignoring the task of fruit.
Would so many poems rise from steam and,
suds and peelings if not for this window,
fences, fields of chickory beyond it?
Were there tiles instead—pragmatic grids—my
thoughts might fling against them, with the thud of
wings trying to kiss their glass reflection.
Yet this might not have been my home at all.
I'd been through so many homes—with skylights,
stained-glass windows, glossy trapezoids or
octagons—with other men inside them.

Borrowing Your Shower

Naked, here, where you are daily naked,
my flesh feels apt to bloom,
fragility watering my leafiness,
my toes rooting to your bathtub bottom.

And if you burst in with hands full of blackberries,
how could I not nuzzle them
from your chalice palms with my wet mouth?

My own water is never this hot, never fizzles
as if giggled from a clown's seltzer bottle.

And if a photographer should splash
the wide wings of me with light,
how could I refuse to still, to pose?

Your mirror flashes me myself in silver dampness,
and there is, somewhere, a piccolo,
armloads of peonies, and nectarines—sliced thinly,
spread across a shortbread tart shell, glistening.

Cutting-Off Ears

We watched this show on TV about a painter who slowly went mad, and about his wife who stayed with him, bathed him with moistened cloths, kept gawkers at from the porch and windows. And I slid my hand on his belly, felt movings under the skin, said, *will you still love me when I'm a crazy writer?* and I smiled and so did he, but only a little. *Will you be...* he said, pressing my hand, and his belly grumbled, *will you be a crazy writer?* and somehow, I took it as a dare.

Translations from the English into Admissions of Everyday Fears

When she says:

See you later,

what she means is:

Sometimes the breeze tries to fray my muscles.

When she says:

I'm tired today,

what she means is:

To cut into an under-ripe cantaloupe is a failure.

When she says:

Pick up some milk on the way home, will you?

what she means is:

My shoes feel like they're from my childhood closet.

When she says:

The mail is late,

what she means is:

If only the baby bunnies never had to fear dogs.

When she says:

Hold me,

what she means is:

...or else I might dissipate like smoke.

When she says:

Look! A heron,

what she means is:

Someday, everyone will leave.

October Morning

Left bare toes
standing cold on right ones
on concrete porch,
she watched his car
puff-smoke away,
thought, *muffler needs fixed,*
pulled yellow terry robe
close to her thin waist,
thought *he'll be back,*
be back, be back.
She swore she saw
black shadows swirl-moving
in those prettiest of
morning pink sun streaks
through trees, reaching,
on barely-frosted grass,
swore they were closer
at each breath,
moving in.
She stepped inside, shut door
tight with both arms,
leaning into it.

October Afternoon

In the field behind her house,
flocks bled upward, outward,
black feather trellis
stretching to thin strip clouds
in gray sky.
She sunk down, squinted
to blur the bird lines,
wavering stain raised
left then right from the dead
of brown-dry feed corn,
unified, as if attached to
each other's oil-dark tail-fans.
She hugged her rough knees
to her chest, breathed leaf-air,
waiting for the birds to
decide on a direction,
knowing they will leave south,
feeling she might be pulled,
stitched to their wings.

October Night

She smelled fire,
searched out windows
for which neighbor burned,
finding an orange pile glow
in the distance
opening a red-yellow hole
in blue night,
breathing ash-flame life
into cold star air.
She wondered what she would
burn, if she had to.
Everything she had, she needed—
couch, afghan, books.
Her hair, she thought.
She could spare some
to sizzle singe however briefly.
Toe and fingernails.
They'd burn.
And her tonsils, appendix,
one kidney, a few feet of
intestine, artery, vein.

She had enough

to let go,

to light a bit of dark for once,

to stand near amongst smoke and glow

and warm what's left of her.

To a Friend Who Moved to Florida II

We know blizzards—their white
oblivion beyond our windows.

You cowered in your girlhood basement while
a tornado growled over your house.

We know broken
glass and fences,
blackout, flood and lightning.

But this—
this hurricane Irma wider than your Florida
dangling into hot fuel ocean like
a child's stray toe tempting under-bed monsters—
this is new.

This could swallow your new life,
take you further from me
than you already flew.

You wait, collect
batteries, water bottles,

shutter windows with dark steel for

three days of waiting in dark.

I watch swirl-color CNN maps

trace projected paths with

fingertip on the screen

resting there

your town below my fingertip, shielded.

Dear Abby,

What should I take—having permission to
dig from my dead friend's garden?

If I try the tall ironweed
I will cry if my winds blow it over.

I could stick to sweet clover—
exotic in my weed-less suburb lawn.

If milkweed, and if monarchs come,
in that way she would hover near.

The tulip blooms are weeks gone now,
so I wouldn't know colors til spring.

In that way she would surprise.
The way her death was a surprise.

Perhaps it's best to avoid surprise.
If I try a lily, it might disappear into mine.

If I transplant strawberries, and bluejays

eat them, in that way I will have failed her.

Tell me which she would choose,
were she here to choose,

to trowel it out herself,
plop it in a plastic grocery sack,

hand it to me on my front porch, saying,
Here.

This would look nice over there.
To brighten your shade.

Two Towers

My sister was deep in the brown middle
of Kansas when 9/11

happened, the highways
narrow and cell service

spotty, and my mother desperate
to know she was safe, desperate

to tell her what was happening, while
afraid for her to know how evil

men had managed to take the world
by surprise. My sister's car rolled

west, her much-older boyfriend asleep
in the passenger seat,

her few boxes of clothes and
Goodwill second-hand

chairs dragged in a rental trailer over

highway roadkill.

There would be a shabby apartment
in LA that my mother would never visit.

Then another, when my sister
squirrelled-away enough tips

in a shoebox to leave while
he slept. My mother needed to tell

her about the towers, needed her to know
how even the strong can one day explode.

Gone

When his wife of thirty years left,
taking only two suitcases—
packed while he was at work,
hefted to her Buick trunk under drizzle,
returning two days later
with her brothers for the rest—
he told himself he'd make the best of it.

Instead he stumbled, squinting, bracing on
the arm of the sofa, hollowed dresser
drawers, refusing now to open
miniblinds and curtains in the morning,
his home now strange and overbright.

Like a blind man suddenly sighted,
re-learning his dark, textured world,
that now flings illuminated color
swaths at his face from every angle,
finding respite only at night,
he focused on familiar, enduring sounds—
the neighbor's bamboo windchimes,
cicadas, car engines closer closer gone.

When Drinking Alone, the Mind Ponders Unknowable Things

Which different turn of a ten-year-old's bicycle
might have lead to an entirely different
lifelong string of lovers.

The exact proportion of water to sand for castling,
not sprinkling away to nothings,
not landsliding to shapeless sludge.

My last words to my father.
His to me.

Why a deteriorated rope hangs from
a dead tree in the downtown scraggly cliff
edge of the Maumee River.
Surely no tire swing.

Even last-ish words might suffice.
There must have been a phone call.
Hey. Pause.
Is Mom home?

Lyrics for a melody stuck

replaying staggered bits of itself

behind my eyebrows,

beyond cumulonimbus clouds,

beneath the dirt's named strata.

What I do wrong each time I mix an Old Fashioned,

each bartender doing it differently,

better than the last, so I keep letting them,

keep going.

Oz

Mamma always told me to think about Oz—when brownish things stopped me from sleeping without the hall light on, or when my brother punched me in the upper arm, leaving marks, because I touched his stuff. Mamma said Oz would pull me whispering to it, like a woman flirting with her open mouth, make me sleep, make me remember the emerald thrills of being far from home—the different-smelling pillows, boarding passes inked with circular stamps—make me remember the blood rush of craving to return.

Northwest, Flight 2-0-Something

Two by two, they boarded willingly,
nudging from behind or being nudged
by someone just like them.
The cow comforted through
romping waves and shrieking bats
by the musk of her bull.
The buck tucking his doe
between his forelegs,
antlers guarding against rats and thunder.

The animals licked salt water seeping
through cracks in old planks,
ignoring each other's messes and
muscles shrunk from disuse,
ignoring illness and
dustiness of sleep, of sex,
because, above all else,
they had a two for their one,
a same amongst strangers.

And as you fly away again tonight,
you leave me, the she-dove

a one now amongst twos,

awaiting her husband's return

and news of dry land.

Late Night Supper

After a long long hot spring workday
with my husband, some
sweat-stressed hollering in the work truck,
I flipped on the backyard light,
stirred mushrooms,
red pepper hunks—
oiled on a slip of foil—
and Italian sausage links
on the grill.

The neighbors all had finished
making love, were now
brushing teeth, contemplating
whether to keep windows open overnight,
or shut them against maybe storms.

Heat lightning pulsed across
eastern cloudbanks.
I sniffed the air for new ozone, for
if I needed more garlic,
watched thunderless lightning—
woeful without its rumbles—

strained to hear spring peepers over

my sizzle,

to see dark flight shadows in

the blackblue clouded sky.

I wondered if I should go in

and tell my husband

supper was nearly done,

or let the scent through the window

tell him for me.

The Last Day of June

We met twenty-two
years ago this week. Tonight's moon

is full and nicotine-stained.
They say

tonight Venus and Jupiter
are nearer to each other

than at any other blip
in their twenty-four year orbits—

dual bleach blots in denim, western
sky. It occurred

to you to
lower the shade midway through

sex, though no one could see in
our high window. And

anyway

it was too late

if some backyard astronomer
telescoping Venus and Jupiter

or golden moon lakes might
have magnified,

at fifty-times-power, twinned planetary
bodies—their gravities

impelling them near and away and near
and away and near.

Satisfaction

Days past turning thirty-five,

in the coffee shop

my cup is bland.

From the window I see

a sun-bronzy bum lift

a cigarette butt from

the weather-cracked parking lot

of the Salvation Army thrift store.

He glances in the store window,

strolling past,

eyes up, maybe wishing.

I pretend to read while

unable to ignore

a dull conversation behind me.

The wooden seat is hard

against my thighs.

The air conditioning blasts away

the gorgeous steamy July,

and I wonder if the bum

tastes the asphalt

along with the nicotine and tar,

if the filter is damp, still, from

a stranger's mouth,

if he found himself a light,

if the smoke winds upward through

his wiry white mustache hairs

to his nose, satisfying

a little something in him.

To My Husband's Honda

I did not mean to punch your dashboard,

to smash my fist through its thin plastic shell,

exposing your dials and tiny wand hands

that indicate the levels of your engine liquids.

But the dash would not light up—

you, in your old age, refusing to behave as expected,

like when the driver's side window, on a Wednesday,

will not raise up at the touch of its button, or

how the heater will only blow at full force,

rejecting subtlety in favor of

shouting its warmth in my face.

When your dash did not light up, dark

at the late-night, downtown curbside,

I felt abandoned, driving deserted grimy streets

at unknown speeds, unsure of my fuel level,

you secreting your insides from me entirely.

I meant only to knock you,

to jiggle whatever had come loose, whatever

had frayed and lazily diffused itself inside you.

But lacking depth perception in the dark,

and panicking in the shadowy dilapidated haze,

instead my fist smashed through the flimsy clear

covering, revealing your silly mechanisms

as the hand-assembled bits of plastic they are,

and nicking the skin of my knuckle,

drawing a seep of blood to suck away,

as if violence had occurred instead of fear.

To the Bicycles

I mutter cursewords at your paint-chipped bones
entangled in the garage periphery,
blocking the recycling bins and scrapwood
and plastic lawn chairs and
whatever else I need to reach.
Five bicycles in gradating sizes,
at times leaning precariously against
each other like a pair of half-felled trees,
or lying, your wheel under the car's rear tire.
You are there, always, underfoot,
your metal webs flopped against my
necessary piles of junk instead of
perched properly on your kickstands.
But then again your kickstands likely are bent,
unusable. Your seats in need of adjustment for
whichever legs fit you this month,
your chains might be disengaged, awaiting
daddy to fix them, your tires spongy.

I am sorry for cursing your bruises to my shins
as I shimmy past you with grocery bags or
trash cans headed for the curb.

After all, your arthritic, rusted mechanicals
will be needed for only a short while longer—
brief years of zipping over sidewalks
behind shinier bikes bought from
sporting-goods stores instead of garage sales.
Years of having your brittle handgrips peeled
by absentminded small hands in June sun,
of being dropped to driveways,
of being polka-dotted with fingernail polish,
of lying on the lawn in warm rainshowers,
of whisking children, only the few yards away
from me that their thighs and I can handle.

Holding Someone Else's Baby

I give him what I can,
and it's enough, because
he expects nothing of me.

My voice is a new music,
as if drifted through a
June window.

Our faces, a haze of unrelated
features to gaze at,
without milk or lesson.

We are each other's candy—
briefly intoxicating
and flimsy, and

nourishing home can be had
later, after
the afternoon's sleep.

Absorbing Milk from an Overturned Glass

I can read my poems aloud to my babies.
Or sing to them—
right at their glinting globe eyes—
assuming their gelatin brains make
some kind of sense of it all,
signals bouncing through the gel
from peach hunk to grape half,
forming ideas about rhythm and
the various uses for lips and tongues.
As they age, though, I am wary of
the wisdom beyond their stares—
doubting my tales of Santa or Jesus,
or craning their necks to see tears
on my cheeks before I crush them
against my hunched shoulders.
I want to know them—
to be able to choose a book
from the shelf, confident it is one
they will love, will gasp for.
To be able to place a plate of food
in front of their forked fists
that sets their saliva glimmering.

To be able to welcome their aging brains

into my outstretched arms

like a peony's fluttered petals

roiling with parties of ants.

Like table linen, rushed,

absorbing milk from an overturned glass.

To know them, but without

threat of reciprocation.

For My Daughter, On Valentine's Day

My heart burrows under piles
of blankets squeezing itself

dark, as you swell and round and blush,
awaiting love

like you read in books, and sweat
and even teardrops—not knowing yet

how they will dissolve you. Young
hearts break. Old hearts only brown

brittle from the edges like pages
of old books. I will have to watch

you rupture, your wounds re-opening my
own—from heart and belly

and breast—and I can't
prevent it any more than

I could prevent your slick crush from
womb to bright room.

My hope, at least, is that I'm gone
before your pages begin to brown.

Driving Lesson

Our friends sold us the car, but
even shampooed seats and floormats
hasn't rinsed away the smell
of their grief
and of their dog, long dead.

My teenage son now
in the passenger seat.
Out my driver-side window
a bald eagle's head and tail
electrify white against blue sky.
Look, an eagle, I say

otherwise quiet. I don't lecture
about driving lessons—
how he can't hide below roofs forever.

The dog used to droop his jowls
out the window, slobber trailing and
streaking the sky-blue paint.

A small bird pecks and swoops
at the eagle's dark back.

Why does it dare?

No one should want to hurl themselves
into an object in motion,
to propel oneself at 70mph
over unending asphalt.

Every time I slip into this car
I smell the dog I didn't even like
and remember stroking its bristly hide.
It didn't know its last car ride
was its last.

Ahead, paired black streaks
on pavement S themselves toward
the right-side ditch.

What makes a dog ever-willing
to thrust his whole head
out moving car windows? To inhale
wind enough to hinder breath?

No one wants to close a door and
walk away, knowing it will never

open again. Except when they do.

I don't know if my son turned
to watch the eagle, and if so
if he was rooting for the little bird,
or afraid for it.

Withholding

(Mark Rothko, Untitled 1960, Mixed Media on Canvas, Toledo Museum of Art.)

Rothko's planes of layered pigments barely press
toward each other like teenaged thighs—inadvertently
but controlledly aligning in football bleachers.
Like china cabinet wine glasses hovering,
not clinking together at footsteps.

My son taps his phone. My onions simmer on the stovetop.
I don't ask if he's ever kissed a girl or boy.
I can't remember for him the first time he gasped
and screamed in sterile hospital air.
I can't press his chest against another to ignite sparks.

Some pigments were never intended to blend, or
would bleed so fully they would transform.
He thinks he knows the risk in transformation.
It's as if Rothko knew I could never say everything,
knew that my son would never boil over, that I
can't remember for him the moment he decided to lean away,
and I can't instead unsteady his balance into me.
Sometimes two beings are bridged only by air carrying
the scent of browning butter. Some bodies coexist,
appreciating, simmering from safe distance, like a dare.

As you are Vasectomized

Thank you seems inappropriate
as you lay still on that cold bed
of your own free will, of course,
as you must, by now, have grown weary
of working long long days with
so many small beings awaiting your return,
awaiting meat, vaccines, cars and college.

As the needles are jabbed, paused, in what
would be your last choice of places,
do you recall epidurals, IVs, episiotomies?
Do you multiply your thirty minutes
by five, by twenty? Do you think me brave?

As you recover, in your usual chair so that
the kids see no real difference, save
my fetching of soda, of Vicodin, of soup,
and save the bag of frozen peas where
men normally crave only heat,
do you recall my slow easing on and off
of chairs, my tentative hikes upstairs
for loads of laundry, toilet scrubs and

my cringing, kneeling over bathtubs full of

slippery, babies then coaxed to bed?

Do you resent the lack of flowers,

of greeting cards and gifts, and nothing

new to snuggle, soft at our breast?

Do you regret losing the maybe-one-more,

the maybe-later? Or fear the loss of those

already yours to sickness, to crashes?

Once they are again mine, I promise

to be good to you and to them, to be gentle

at first like you have been so many months

to my round self, toppled on my side,

and to my tensed, reluctant body, fearing

I'd never return myself completely to you.

Horse Play

Our friends' Florida guest room had been
their nursery—wallpapered in split rail fences

and horses of every color like her back-
home Kentucky. They made it look

easy to gallop away. Daylong our
friends lead us to water, flies caught in hair,

eyeing gators with sense to slink
from airboats. We eat from shells like

in-landers, wander Thomas Edison's summer
home. Your legs stride further

than mine even when headed to the same place.
Two a.m. I straddle you like a hobby horse

shush shush rocking slow, steady friction enough
but avoiding bedframe creaks, like the

difference between an electric arc

and a sinus rhythm. Horses leap fences in dark,

manes moon-brushed in vertical blind stripes.
I blink apology for not being newborn here in this

grown-up feather bed, black eyes startled staring,
the way the Seminole must nightmare

strings of plastic flamingo lights along patio
overhangs and sequin bikini tops in the seaoats.

One day they will strip the wallpaper,
the horse legs and the Everglade runs will be over,

beachside daiquiri bars sparked dark in
no-longer-named hurricanes,

and my thighs will cramp when I try to
hold my weight high above you.

Unworn

I yank four nighties from hangers—
    silky slips too cheap
    to be called negligees,
unworn since my twenties.
I realize they must have
    looked pretty on me once,
like discovering you'd been fed
    cake in your sleep.

So many seamstresses and
    hot machines needling wisps of
    sorbet-colored nylon and black lace
    to fake my body into womanly-ness.
It couldn't have been just my skin
I had prettied-up for men.

When the women of my family
all gifted me bridal shower lingerie
    they were instructing in
    the joy of flimsy beauty
the way a mother blows
    hours of backyard soap-bubbles

with her toddler, saying—
through the float and vanish—
that now is for wasting hours
in pastel distraction.

Now, at forty-three,
I offer only opacity—
    the gift of coverage,
    of cloaking the truth of
    all of me.

What is lingerie but celebration?
What are red-embroidered roses—
what is a silk-cord strap made to
    slip off a shoulder—
what is maribou trimming—
what are seed-pearls stitched
    along a plunging neckline—
what is nylon sheer as July haze—
but gift wrap for
    an offering of youthfulness?

Grandma is Ninety Today

A good long life. And yes
I suppose she is

good. In general. But, how good would we
all try to be if we knew we

would only live to thirty,
instead of ninety

years of accountability, of
children, bosses, neighbors, lovers—

their assessments of our lives.
Who might

we be willing to hurt if we knew
we would be gone soon,

and fewer folks would judge—
too busy saying, *She was so young.*

She had her whole life ahead.

Grandma was not always a good

woman. Smirking,
once, admitting

that every gift ever
received from her daughters

had been stashed in an attic corner.
Or retreating to a campground for

gray weeks alone when
aunt Linda got pregnant at sixteen.

If there had been
only a decade ahead,

might Grandma
have been willing to kick Aunt Linda

out. Or to hand back the earrings,
blouses, and magazine

subscriptions, say, *No thank you.*

The nurse delivers pink balloons

to Grandma's room, ties the ribbons
on her metal bedrail. They bobble in

fluorescent light,
and Grandma smiles sweet

as a store-bought cake icing swirls,
asks *who's the birthday girl?*

Of Course

Of course I would never
harm the robin who for

five days has pecked
and fluttered its fur-like breast

against the sliding glass door, despite
his keeping me up most of the night,

and when I do drift off
I dream of roofers

re-shingling above my head.
Of course I loved

my father, and of course he loved me.
Of course regrets do not keep

me up most of the night,
dreaming of how he might

have instead grown into a gray old

man like others have. Of course we know

that if we
hurt something we

will regret it,
so of course we choose not to, but

sometimes do anyway,
and when we

dream at night,
of course we have no control over who's there.

Winter Fight

Despite the way the heft of them resists
everyday winds

every tree is susceptible to lightning,
every rooftop to weight

of snow.
All these radio

lyrics make sense now—
the ones about

love being a bitch, and hearts
obliterated, scarred

and all those wet pillows and bottles
of whiskey. As if all along

they had been yodeling
in foreign tongues and something

gave way inside me,

quit resisting

commonplace awfulness,
realigning with a gasp,

and I understand.
Earthquakes can

split Ohio, even, and frozen
pipes can burst before you know they froze.

December 1st, and You're Away

I climbed into our attic to retrieve bent boxes marked *X-MAS* in black Sharpie. Snowglobes with plastic carolers puckered in one everlasting *Oh,* porcelain nativity with cracked-and-glued cow, years of ceramic and lights and tin to change the mantle, to remind us that snow and the glow of cinnamon candles means us under afghans awaiting something fleeting. But now you are away—returning soon but nonetheless gone—and as I climb the fold-down staircase, I lay my telephone at the base, in case I should fall.

To My Husband's Best Friend

I know I am like the cold moon—
a dark-halved liar who

seems full three days instead of its mere one.
When I am gone,

any woman
could sidle in

to solace the brave widower—
with the bronze moonglow of her.

But you, you could not be replaced—
you and your shared decades

of musing, gripes, and easy joy.
You, the surf to his shore,

tide-ing away then together in
salted cleansing.

Your death

would leave a gulf

I could not fill, and he might
decide to hate me for it.

And should he die,
you and I

might need to make love to conjure him.
Three become two become three again.

You and I and our griefs adhered
to mold a bright sphere

of him from our scant
crescents of remaining light.

Love Song for the Fragile

Our breaks arise differently—
mine either from
having been yanked
or from slow compression.

I still wake in shock that I never
grew up to become Ginger Rogers,
ashamed of my utter lack of
fringe, stiletto tap shoes or moxie.
You do not fault me for this.

There are ways we can splint
each other's fracturing.

Decades ago, when ponded snowmelt
in the back yard froze-over, we
neighbor kids played what we
called hockey with gray tennis balls.
A small girl broke through, and we
formed a chain to pull her from
shin-deep water, as was our duty.

I still wake in shock that never
am I climbed upon
without splintering.

My one crop of deciduous teeth
has long since dropped, like
a pear tree's season wasted
in a foreclosed yard.

There are ways we can jump fences,
climb, rescue abandoned fruit.

The tooth of a megalodon would
fill your man-sized hand entirely.
I have no exoskeleton.
No horns nor scaly hide.

I still wake in shock that you never
have seen me broken.

My parents had a cabinet of glass
fruit and fish, lead crystal decanters
and snifters from years teaching
in war-torn Czechoslovakia.

There are ways to convey
these things so easily destroyed.

I still wake in shock that I never
became unbreakable.

Post-Op (January 2020)

I warm soup for my mother—
tomato from my garden. Her

right kneecap was popped
off like a pill bottle cap,

tendons stretched aside still
clinging to muscle, legbone ends filed

flat, all reassembled with nylon bits
fabricated to keep her upright.

When she asks me to click
Fox News on her TV, I deflect,

suggest the Classic Movie channel—something
gray where men tip fedoras to women

in calf-length dresses. I walk
her to the toilet when she needs. A fall

would easily take us both down.

I refuse to recall the Trump sticker on

her car—the way her
recessed ceiling lights hover

hotly near but not into attic insulation.
These walls and curtains

of my girlhood are shadowed
and still. I refill her water cup cold,

count narcotics and aspirin to her
palm. In three days my sister

will fly here to take over. I hoist the dead
weight of her right leg

into the recliner chair. She says my sister
should have a baby before

it's too late—but not before
she's married. I say she can't afford
birth, maternity leave, pediatrician.
I try to believe that this flesh-and-blood woman

would have sewn my wedding gown
still, were my husband Muslim or Honduran,

or had I married a woman. I bring
in the newspaper, load her body and walker in

the car for physical therapy
where, while strapped to machines,

Trump's impeachment hearing
is muted on TVs. Closed-captioning

and Carole King on Musak. Back home, I click on
something with Cary Grant, and Mom

opens mail—doctor bills with Medicare a tenth
of what I pay with insurance constantly at threat

of being stripped away. She taps
the envelope, says all this and

her surgeon didn't even look American.
Says I better save for retirement.

Her right knee swells into new configuration.
Her left knee, bearing the brunt

must know it is next for dismantling.
Together they will do what she

asks of them. The cat prances between
us in TV light, as if he knows someone

is hurt, someone strange is here,
and things that are amiss eventually return

to normal. The furnace
hum is different since

I left living here, the birdsongs
outside are the same. On

the TV, there is always a chance
the characters might break out into song.

Restless

The sweat of my feet
in the long grass becomes the sweat

of centuries of prairie
women. The dread of the breeze

is the haunt of those pioneers
who survived winters,

planted their squash seeds
and pears and prayed for life and heat

and whatever else may blossom from solid mud.
I am restless in my blood,

as if fearing tornados or mistakes
in judgement, like the way

I used to play
with Bittersweet Nightshade

that strangled the gas

meter at the edge of the yard, mashing

the bitter-tomato-smelling berries
into slimy broth in a Frisbee

full of last night's drizzle.
Its purple

blossoms beaked with pointed yellow
centers, like grizzled old

birds in some Malaysian cave. I never knew
the bright juice

of the plaything on my fingertips
was poison. I am pillow-slipped

in springtime again
somehow, as if steel winter never happened.

I will tend and grow my futile
greens and purples,

as if they won't be dead in months, as if it

benefits streams or aphids

or meadowlarks, as if
any of it might have sense enough

to vine itself
around something strong enough to sustain it.

Mankind

College applications have been sent for
this boy, a head higher than me—
I refuse to say *man* when he was once
the length of my ulna, skull barely a palmful.

If he lived nearer Lake Erie he might
climb shore boulders each morning.

When sunrise is particularly
pomegranate-stained, there is a gulp of hope.
More often day seeps forward muddily
and I doubt mankind as its whole.

This boy—I refuse to say *man* when
his tear ducts were born closed filaments
my pinkie-tip massaged to clear the way for tears.
He will leave home never having
taken a car for an oil change.

Most sunrises are throats willing to choke
mankind down, and most deserve it, and most
wouldn't know how to fight their way out.

If he lived in the desert he might
sleep midday away avoiding heat.

Mankind might be better off if
half of its bodies slept half
their lives away alone.

This boy will leave—I refuse to say *man* when
his penis was once a jelly bean, both feet
could have curled inside a plastic Easter egg.
Will leave home never having
chopped firewood, or scrambled eggs.

Dawn chastises my disappointing mankind,
my filling-out a lifetime of forms,
useless checkboxes, sad data, waiting news of
who will haul a hunk of me away.

If he lived by the ocean he might
never escape my salt.

Timing, Leaves, 2017

Mid-August,
seven monarch

caterpillars in a mesh basket, four
milkweed leaves each morning,

four each night. Five children
in the back of the van,

headphones squeeze-in a specific dose of
the world, muffle the

rest. Their lips move, speaking
to air inside themselves, or singing.

In undramatic cloudless dusk
half of a brown maple leaf falls from

the pages of my estate-sale journal.
If I concentrate, the caterpillars' gradual

munching is my capillaries' labor.

Early September,

seven monarch butterflies released to wind.
Hurricane Harvey liquifies Houston,

four children read in bed-light glow,
thunderstorms shuddering windows.

I mumble John Ashbery, barely aloud
to a glass of twelve-year-old bourbon.

One no-longer-a-child maybe reads, but
I cannot know, far in a dormroom bunk.

Milkweed leaves curl, sag in
the garden as if they know this

thundercould be it. Ashbery has died.
These mumbles will continue until all rain dries

all wings fly. Pages will
turn themselves.

Marblehead

The lighthouse lamp is dark,
and the caretaker's shack—their insides locked,

shuttered from thunder, mayflies,
and the always always

wind. Young, I was willing to teeter on slick seaweedy
boulders, calf-deep

in the cold, Lake Erie side of the waves—
not the calm Sandusky Bay

side of childhood, of railway howls,
of Grandpa's coal-dock towers,

of perch fishing off
Uncle Tom's Lyman. I knew the water dropped off

deep somewhere, hard with earth's cold
minerals. Kelly's Island

on the horizon, with its snakes.

Canada beyond, with caribou and glaciers.

Older now, I would be willing to abandon
my inland

everything, for a post-war bungalow where
families summered away

from the bottle factory, shipyard
and schoolhouse. I would plant a peach orchard,

stitch a kite, allow constant wind and gulls to weave
through my clapboards, gust me

with wet sand and walleye, and wait for
the light to be restored.

Acknowledgements

The author would like to thank the publications in which some of the poems in this collection first appeared:

"Shell" *Poetry Letter* (2004.) "Kitchens Are for Cooking" *Alimentum* (2006.) "October Morning," "October Afternoon," and "October Night" *The Country Mouse* (2006.) "Abstract" *Think Journal* (2009.) "Staying," *Broadway Bards First* (The Poetry Barn Press 2010.) "Tea and Cake" The Toledo Lucas County Public Library website (2011.) "Iceland Green" *Miriam's Well* (2011.) "Satisfaction" *Third Wednesday* (2012.) "Absorbing Milk from an Overturned Glass" and "Bathrooms Are for Bathing" *Journey to Crone* (Chuffed Buff Books 2013.) "Store-Bought Cookies" *Third Wednesday* (2013.) "To the Bicycles," *Midwestern Gothic* (2013.) "To My Husband's Honda," *Third Wednesday*, (2011) and *The Toledo Poetry Project* (2014.) "Late Night Supper," *Slippery Elm* (2014.) "Translations from the English into Admissions of Everyday Fears," *Clockwise Cat* (2014.) "Out the Window" *Slippery Elm* (2014.) "Borrowing Your Shower," *2015 Hessler Street Fair Poetry Anthology* (Crisis Chronicles Press 2015.) "During a Too-Early November Snowfall," and "For My Daughter, On Valentine's Day," *Ohio Poetry Day Anthology* (Ohio Poetry Day Association Press 2015.) "The Last Day of June," *Slippery Elm* (2015.) "To my Husband's Best Friend" *Rat's Ass Review* (2015.) "Marblehead," *Parks and Points* (2017.) "Two Towers," *2017*

Hessler Street Fair Poetry Anthology (Crisis Chronicles Press, 2017.) "Cutting Off Ears," *Resurrection of a Sunflower* (Pksi's Porch Publishing, 2017.) "Pixie Cut," *Slippery Elm* (2017.) "Mankind" *Blue Mountain Review* (2017.) "Dear Abby" *Artifacts* (NightBallet Press 2017.) "Body as Bird as Body" *Common Threads* (Ohio Poetry Association Press 2017) and *isacoustic* (2018.) "2/3 Water" *Paper and Ink* (2018.) "Dysmorphia" *isacoustic* (2018.) "To a Friend Who Moved to Florida II" *Gasconade Review* (2018.) "Spider-man" *Red Fez* (2019.) "Unworn" *Thimble* (2020.) "Driving Lesson" *Slippery Elm* (2020.) "Withholding" Toledo Museum of Art website (2020.) "Restless" *Great Lakes Review* (2020.) "Winter Fight" *Up North Lit* (2020.) "Horseplay" *Mock Turtle Zine* (2020.) "Drops" *Funicular* (2021.) "Stray" *Slippery Elm* (2021.) "When Drinking Alone, the Mind Ponders Unknowable Things" *As it Ought to Be* (2021.) "Absorbing Milk From an Overturned Glass" *The Lake* (2021.) "Love Song for the Fragile," *Many Nice Donkeys* (2021.) "Bathrooms Are For Bathing," *River Dog Zine* (2022.) "Rose Window" and "Post Op (January 2020)," *Red Fez* (2022.) "To a Friend Who Moved to Florida," *Saw Palm* (2022.)

"*Unknowable Things* is seamless start to finish. Not a word wasted, or misplaced. No splinters. Each poem written with stark honesty, unflinching, yet smooth, polished and tender. Trautman masters the art of pulling deeper meaning out of the everyday ordinary, and effortlessly crafts the weight of human existence into poetry that is universal, self-reflective and outright beautiful."—Dan Denton, author of *Finding Jesus & Prayers to my Saints*

"*Unknowable Things* reads as if you're holding a personal notebook that has somehow accidently been misplaced, only to wind up in your hands. Should you be reading Kerry Trautman's personal notebook? Yes? No? You know, they say that there is excitement and enjoyment that comes from doing things that you know you shouldn't do...so do it...get excited and enjoy how Trautman writes with a laid bare honesty that's crafted and at times sharp enough to cut deep to the bone, like a sliver of a broken mirror that we can all see small pieces of our own reflections in. Trust me, it's a beautiful thing."—Victor Clevenger, author of *47 Poems*